CW00746198

DIARY

OF A
MINECRAFT
ENDERMAN

BOOKS KID

TABLE OF CONTENTS

Day 1

Last night I had a dream, a dream I've had a few times before. There's my name, up in lights: *Eli Enderman.* Hordes of endermen are shouting and cheering waiting for me to appear.

Suddenly, there I am, appearing in the middle of the stage as if by magic. A single spotlight follows me as I start to sway in time to the music before bursting into song.

I jolt awake from the nightmare. No, not the fact I was singing on stage, but what happened after the show. The audience started booing, hating my performance, despite having been so excited about it.

My name is Eli Enderman and I have a big secret. I want to be a famous singer.

I have never told another living soul about my secret. There's a good reason why you've never heard of any famous Enderman singers. Normally, we're quite shy and retiring creatures. That's why most of us hate being stared at and attack anyone who dares to look at us for too long.

In Enderman society, it's very rude to stare.

But I'm different. I *like* it when people look at me. I *like* being the center of attention.

My love of music first started when some Minecraftians came to The End. They were sitting around a campfire, trying to keep warm and safe while they plotted to slay the Ender Dragon. I heard them singing a song together and I couldn't resist moving towards them. I'd never heard anything like it before.

This is the end, they sang. *We're at the end of the world and it's the end of everything we know. Winds blow and fires glow, water flows but nothing grows in the end.*

It was a haunting tune, made even more beautiful when one of them added a little harmony.

I could have stood there listening to them forever, but a Minecraftian saw me coming. Scrambling to his feet, he grabbed a bow and shot an arrow in my direction, leaving me no choice but to teleport away.

I never forgot the song I heard, though.

Day 2

I can't stop thinking about my dream. Would the other Endermen really hate it if I started singing?

There's only one way to find out. I decided to go and sing to one of my friends. Well, I say friends. Endermen don't really have friends, even though we like to stick together. It's just that the more Endermen there are, the harder it is to attack us. We're one of the most misunderstood creatures in Minecraftia. Just because we live in The End and we know the Ender Dragon, Minecraftians assume we're evil and we want to fight.

I just want to put it in writing that we're not *that* evil. OK, we like a good fight – who doesn't? But we don't go out actively looking for trouble. Start a fight with us and we'll finish it, but leave us alone and we're more than happy to ignore you.

Anyway, if a group of Endermen are wandering around, it's usually enough to frighten off any potential attackers, so we can go about our business peacefully. After all, only an idiot would take on a group of us.

I remember the last time one such idiot came to The End. He was armed with a whole heap of enchanted weapons and thought this would be enough to kill us all. Mad fool.

Picture the scene. A Minecraftian walks straight into The End and yells "Come on, then! Who's bad enough to fight me?"

Of course, we all ignored him, so he pulled out his sword. He then walked straight up to Bert, my brother, and stared him straight in the face.

That was it. Bert started shaking with rage, too angry to do anything at first, until the Minecraftian whacked him on the head with his sword.

Letting off a loud Enderman war cry, Bert ran straight at him, teleporting all around until the Minecraftian didn't know which way to turn. Hearing the sound of battle, I rushed in to help Bert, joined by the other Endermen in the area and the Minecraftian found himself trying to fend off eight Endermen at once.

He didn't stand a chance.

I would love to be able say that after what happened, nobody else dared to mess with us, but the problem with being such efficient fighters is that Minecraftians aren't exactly in a position to be telling anyone anything about how frightening we are.

It's hard to talk when you've been killed.

Day 3

The memories of fighting that Minecraftian have given me an idea, an idea that I can't stop thinking about, even though I've been shaking my head, trying to shake it out.

When we worked together, it was a beautiful sight, almost like a ballet, as a whole group of Endermen came together in perfect harmony for one common goal. What if I could get a group of Endermen to choreograph a song and dance number?

I know it might sound daft, but the more I think about it, the more amazing it could be. We could sell tickets for the show, invite all of Minecraftia to come and then everyone will see that we're peaceful really, so they'd all leave us alone instead of trying to attack us. And with all the money we make, we could build a theater in The End! We could put on shows all the time then.

They might even name it after me as a little thank you. The Eli Enderman Theater has a real ring to it, don't you think?

The first step will be to find some other Endermen who want to be in my show. I can't be the only one here who wants to sing. If I could find three other Endermen, we could put together a barber shop quartet. Imagine the harmonies we'd create together. Minecraftia will never have heard anything like it. We'll go down in history! We'll be famous!

I have to find other Endermen who like singing and fast.

Day 4

It's proving harder than I thought it would be to find other Endermen who want to be in my show. They're all so boring. None of them can think outside of the box.

"Too busy!" one said.

"Haven't got time!" said another.

"Leave me alone. Can't you see I'm building a box?" a third one said.

It was very depressing.

I slumped down against an obsidian pillar, wondering whether I could train my voice to sing more than one part at the same time.

I tried. You don't want to know what it sounded like. No, really. You don't.

My dream was destroyed before it had even had a chance to grow. Who wants to see a show with one Enderman?

"Pssst! Are you the Enderman looking for someone to sing with?"

I looked around, but couldn't see who was speaking.

"Up here." I looked up to see an Enderman perched on top of the column. He looked left and right to make sure that nobody was watching him before jumping down to stand next to me.

"So? Are you the Enderman who wants to sing?"

I nodded glumly. "I am, but nobody wants to sing with me."

"That's because they're all cowards," he spat. "In our hearts, *all* Endermen want to sing. They just haven't got the courage to admit it. I thought I was the only one who dreamed of performing on stage."

"You have the dream too?" I couldn't believe what I was hearing. This was amazing!

"What dream?" The Enderman looked at me as though I was crazy. "I just meant that I think about it a lot."

"Oh." I blushed. Clearly, I was the only one who had actual dreams of being a star.

"Anyway, if you needed someone to sing with, I'd love to join you."

"Really?" I couldn't believe it. Two Endermen could make beautiful music together!

"Sure! It would be fun. A lot more fun than wandering around The End looking for ways to make the Ender Dragon think I'm being useful."

We looked at each other and shuddered. The Ender Dragon was well known for being very cruel towards Endermen he didn't think were working hard enough. He'd been known to burn Endermen to a crisp just because they looked like they were walking too slowly, even though they were going as fast as they could.

There was so little to do in The End it was difficult to think of productive things to do with our time. There wasn't much to mine and our island wasn't exactly big.

But two Endermen together? We could pretend we were patrolling or practicing our fighting skills when really we were plotting our show.

"Great. My name is Eli," I told him.

"And I'm Philip," came the reply. "But you can call me Phil."

Just like that, our little band began. Things were starting to come together!

Day 5

"What do you think you're doing?"

Phil and I jumped at the sound of the voice. We'd been trying to write a song together, but it's harder than you might think.

My heart sank when I saw who was speaking. Zach was one of the nastiest Endermen around. Most of us don't like fighting, but Zach loves it. He's always the first to join in when there's a battle with a Minecraftian. He's mean too. He always calls me names and I'm never quick enough to come up with a funny reply.

"Not a lot," Phil replied, hoping that Zach hadn't heard our attempts at harmony.

"Looks like it," Zach sneered. "Funny, though. It looked a lot to me like you were trying to write a song."

Phil and I looked at each other, pained expressions on our faces. This was the worst thing that could have happened.

If Zach knew we were planning a show, we'd never heard the end of it.

"Yeah, well, what if we were?" I shrugged, trying to pretend that it was no big deal. "It's not against Enderman law to write songs." Although now that I'd said it, I started to wonder. Maybe it was! Maybe that's why nobody wanted to join in.

"I just figured you could use some help. From what I could hear, your song wasn't exactly great and I have lots of lyrics you could use."

"You've got lyrics?" Phil and I spoke together, unable to believe what we were hearing. Zach, the biggest, baddest Enderman around was a songwriter??

"Lyrics that *you* wrote?" I went on.

"Sure. I spend all my spare time writing songs. I could do with some help with the tunes, but if you need words, I've got plenty of them to go round."

Phil and I didn't know what to say, so we just stared at him.

"What? Did you really think you were the only Endermen who liked singing?"

"Well, yes," I admitted.

"Typical Eli. You always did think you were something special."

And *that* was the Zach I knew. Still, if he had songs for us to sing, that could be really useful and maybe with Zach on our side, the other Endermen would take us more seriously. People didn't like to fight with him. He always won, and he fought dirty too.

"Stay here and I'll go fetch my notebook."

Zach disappeared off to get his songs, leaving Phil and I looking at each other, still unable to believe this was really happening.

"Are we sure it's such a good idea letting Zach join us?" Phil asked eventually.

"What choice do we have?" I replied. "You know what he's like. If we tell him we don't want him around, he's more than capable of getting the other Endermen to laugh at us when we put on our show or worse – he might put on his own show and then nobody will come to our show."

"I suppose so," shrugged Phil. "I just wish that he hadn't heard us. I don't like him very much."

"Neither do I. Still, you never know. It might not be as bad as we think."

Day 6

Zach has an amazing singing voice! Phil and I couldn't believe our ears when he first started singing. I'd hate him even more than I already do if he wasn't so good.

"Do you see what I mean?" he said when he'd finished singing the first verse of one of his songs to us. "I'm not very good at writing tunes, am I?"

"Are you kidding?" I said. "That was amazing!"

Zach blushed. "You're just saying that because you're afraid I'm going to beat you up."

"No, I'm not," I assured him. "Well, yes I am." I shuddered at the memory of the last time Zach had hit me. It really hurt. "But even so. Your voice is incredible and that song was really good. You need to teach it to me and Phil."

He handed us some sheets of paper with the words written on them.

Don't you know who I am?

I'm an Enderman

Just try to understand

I'm an Enderman

And you can't keep me down

"This is how it goes." Zach sang one line and Phil and I repeated it back to him. It was a simple melody and we soon picked it up, Phil and I experimenting with different harmonies to complement Zach's tune.

It didn't take long before we had a brilliant song, the three of us closing our eyes and swaying in time to the music as we lost ourselves in the tune.

I hadn't wanted Zach to be part of our group, but it looks as though we got lucky when he overheard our singing.

Day 7

Zach brought along some other song sheets today and we set to work learning the new material. If we keep going like this, we'll have a complete show in no time! I wonder where we should put up the stage? I wonder whether the other Endermen will even be interested in seeing us sing?

So many questions. So much to do.

"All right, lads. Let's go over *Endermen forever* one more time. One… two… three… four…"

The three of us started singing the soulful ballad about an Enderman who wanted to live forever.

"What do you think you're doing?"

Oh no. Oh no, no, no. That was the voice no Enderman wanted to hear coming up behind them.

The three of us stood as still as statues, as if we could pretend that we weren't real in the hope that he'd go away.

"I asked you a question. What are you doing?"

Slowly, we turned round to face the Ender Dragon who'd crept up behind us. I looked at Phil. Phil looked at Zach. Zach looked at me, indicating with his head that I should be the one to say something.

Thanks, Zach.

"Er… we were just trying out some new war cries. You know, so that if any Minecraftians came to The End, we could scare them away with the terrible noise."

The Ender Dragon laughed. "Much as I agree with you that it's a terrible noise, something tells me you're not telling the truth, so I'll give you one more chance or you'll be Enderman toast."

I gulped. I didn't want to be toast.

"We're singing some songs."

"That's what I thought. And might I ask why, exactly?"

I took a deep breath.

"We thought that it might be a good idea to put on a show for you and all the other Endermen. You know, brighten things up a bit. You have to admit that it is a bit dull and depressing around here."

The Ender Dragon nodded slowly. "Good idea. It's been a long time since there's been any kind of decent entertainment around here. The last time anything fun happened was when that bunch of Minecraftians thought they could get a dragon egg. I soon showed them, though, didn't I?"

All three of us nodded rapidly. The Minecraftians hadn't stood a chance.

"Right. Well, then, I shall expect to see the best show The End has ever seen at the end of the month. You can build a stage just over there. Make sure there's somewhere very comfortable for me to sit. I want the best view in the house."

"Yes sir." The three of us spoke together as the Ender Dragon flapped his wings and flew away.

"Come on, guys! This is just what we wanted, isn't it?" Zach did his best to look on the bright side.

"Yes, but the Ender Dragon? At our first show? Talk about pressure." Phil was pale with nerves.

"Then let's not make it our first show," I said. "Let's go to Minecraftia and find some people to watch us, let us know if we're good enough to perform for the Ender Dragon."

"And if we're not?"

"We will be. We have to be."

Day 8

I don't know whether it's just the pressure of knowing we have to put a show together for the end of the month, but our rehearsals today were awful. Phil was all out of key and Zach kept forgetting the words, even though he was the one who wrote them. If this is what we're like at the thought of people watching us, what will we be like when there's an actual audience?

"Enough!" I cried eventually. "We're better than this. I know we are. What's wrong with you guys?"

"It's just the thought of the Ender Dragon watching," wailed Phil. "What if he doesn't like our songs? We'll be burnt toast!"

"Well if this is how you're going to sing, there's no way he'll like our songs," snapped Zach. "I've never heard someone sing so badly."

"Yeah, well at least I know all my words," countered Phil.

"Stop it, you two!" I stepped between them, seeing that this was about to get ugly. "What's that they say when you're nervous about getting up in front of people? Imagine them all in their underwear!"

"The Ender Dragon doesn't wear underwear, dummy," pointed out Zach.

"So pretend that he does! Use your imagination."

Phil and Zach looked dubious.

"We don't have a choice here. The Ender Dragon wants to see a show, so we're going to give him one. Let's start again and get it right this time. One, two, three, four!"

It was no good. We were even worse now.

"All right, guys. Let's quit for today," I suggested. "Maybe if we all just get a good night's sleep, we'll do better in the morning."

"Yeah," agreed Zach. "That's all it is. We're just tired. We'll be fine after we get some rest."

The three of us went our separate ways, but I know that we were all starting to panic at the thought of what we'd got ourselves into.

Day 9

"You know what the problem is?" We were having another disastrous rehearsal and Zach was becoming increasingly frustrated.

"What?" I asked.

"We need a fourth member of our group. All the best bands have four members. The Spider Jockees. The Rolling Iron Golems. Steve and the Skeletons."

Phil and I looked at each other, nodding. "He's right, you know," said Phil. "A fourth member would make all the difference."

"But who would want to join the band now?" Word had spread that the Ender Dragon wanted us to perform and I'd had a lot of people come up to congratulate me on our success – and tell me that they're glad they weren't going to be on stage with us. Everyone seemed to think that the highlight of our show would be watching us go up in flames when the Ender Dragon had had enough.

"We'll just have to go into Minecraftia and see if we can find another Enderman up there."

Phil and I looked at Zach. It sounded so simple, but none of us had been up to Minecraftia. Who knows what horrors were waiting for us there?

"I hate to say it, but he's right." Phil shrugged. "And if we don't find anyone, going into Minecraftia gives us another option."

"You don't mean-?"

"That's right." Phil nodded. "Running away and hiding."

It was not exactly an Enderman's usual strategy, but when it came to the Ender Dragon, it might be our only hope of survival.

Still, the thought of leaving The End forever was one that sent shivers down my spine. This was my home. Endermen didn't fit in well in the Overworld, although sometimes a few brave souls went up there to explore.

Who'd have thought that my dream of singing would take me all over the world?

Day 10

It's a little known secret that Endermen can create special portals to get out of The End. It's an extension of our teleportation ability. We don't do it very often. Why would we, when The End contains everything we could possibly need?

Still, there are some Endermen who have restless spirits and like to explore the world and that's why I went to find Davey. Davey was one of the most famous Endermen explorers and he'd just returned from a trip to Minecraftia.

"So you want to learn all about the Overworld, do you? What exactly do you need to know?"

I scratched my head. How could I explain to Davey that I wanted to go to Minecraftia to find an Enderman who wanted to be part of my band and who hadn't heard that this would mean almost certain death when we sang in front of the Ender Dragon.

"I guess I want to know where the best places for Endermen to go are," I said weakly. "I mean, you must have seen some amazing things in your travels. What would you say are the places I need to see if I wanted to have the holiday of a lifetime?"

"That's hard to say," Davey replied after a moment's thought. "I suppose it depends on what you're interested in. If you're looking for a fight, then head west. There are a lot of villages over there full of Minecraftians and iron golems. You can spend all day in combat if you want to. If pretty views are more your thing, go east. There's some beautiful countryside in the savannah. South you'll find an extensive network of abandoned mines where there's still treasure to be found if you know where to look. And if you try going north, you can work on your suntan in the desert."

West sounded like it was the best place for me to go, but there was one problem. "What if I don't want to fight anyone? What if…" My voice trailed off as I tried to think of how to explain my dilemma to Davey.

"Let me guess. You want to find someone fool enough to join your show."

I blushed and nodded. "You got me."

"Endermen are pretty rare in the Overworld, and you know how quickly word travels. You'll be lucky to find anyone to join in your madcap scheme. All I can suggest is that you follow your nose. Maybe the gods will be smiling on you and you'll get what you need."

"Thanks, Davey." I left him to go and start packing some supplies for the Overworld. He hadn't exactly given me any confidence in being able to find another Enderman, but you never knew. Strange things can happen in Minecraftia. I'd even heard a story the other day about a wither who thought he was a witch.

Imagine that!

Day 11

Zach, Phil, and I looked at each other, a nervous knot forming in the pit of my stomach.

"Are we ready to do this, boys?" I asked.

Zach and Phil nodded.

"Then let's go!"

Closing my eyes, I focused on opening up a portal to Minecraftia. I felt dizzy as I could sense the world around me starting to spin and dissolve.

There was a strange noise, like an explosion in reverse. I opened my eyes to see that we were somewhere I'd never been before.

"So this is Minecraftia," said Zach, looking around and nodding slowly. "It's very weird. Look at the sky. What a strange color!"

It was strange, a light blue, with a big bright round thing hanging in the middle. "I guess that must be the sun," Phil said, pointing at it. "This is so weird!"

The three of us gazed round, open mouthed as we took in our surroundings. I'd heard that Minecraftia was very different when compared to The End, but I hadn't realized just how different until we'd come here. No wonder there weren't many Endermen up in the Overworld. It is much nicer back at home. Everything is so bright and colorful here. It's so much nicer being surrounded by black and darkness.

We decided to head west, where we were most likely to find lots of people and possibly Endermen. The sooner we find someone to join our little group, the sooner we can get back home. We still have a theater to build and there's not that much time to get everything together for the end of the month.

It's enough to make me want try to find somewhere to hide up here, but I can't let Zach and Phil down. We're a team now and we're going to make this work.

Day 12

"We need to practice our songs as well as find another Endermen, you know," Zach pointed out the next morning after we'd had some breakfast. Raw chicken. Not exactly the best food to start the day, but it was all we could find.

"All right," I agreed. "Let's go through some songs now. Shall we start with *The End, The End, My Beautiful Home*?"

I knew that Phil and Zach were missing home as much as I was from the soul they were putting into the words. "Well done, lads," I told them when we'd finished. "Sing like that for the Ender Dragon and he's going to love us."

"Let's do *Watch out, there's an Endermen about* next," suggested Phil. The upbeat number was one of my favorites and we'd started putting together a snappy dance routine to go with it.

Just as we turned to face the back of the stage for the start of the number, we noticed some Minecraftians watching us.

I could feel Zach and Phil starting to tremble with rage next to me, but I couldn't tell them to calm down because I was shaking too much myself.

"Wait! No! We were just enjoying listening to the music!" cried one of them, but it was too late. The three of us charged at them, making short work of the Minecraftians.

When the fight was over, Zach, Phil, and I looked at each other.

"Do you think we should have done that?" asked Phil. "They did just say that they were enjoying our songs."

"Our first real audience and we slaughtered them," said Zach glumly.

I looked at the poor, fallen Minecraftians. "I suppose the only good thing about this is that they said that they liked our music. Still, we're going to have to work on that whole not-killing-the-audience thing."

I hadn't thought about that, but I should really have taken into account the fact that it's an Enderman's natural instinct to attack when we're being watched. That's something we're going to have to work on for the show, especially if we want to take it touring all over Minecraftia.

"Come on, then," I said. "Let's get moving. Maybe we'll meet someone we can ask about other Endermen. Just remember that if someone starts to watch us *don't* attack them! We need help from these people, and they can't help us if we've killed them all."

"Don't attack people," nodded Phil.

"Got it," nodded Zach.

Day 13

We walked all day yesterday and didn't see any sign of other Endermen. This is going to be a lot harder than I thought. We could spend the rest of our lives wandering around Minecraftia and not find anyone to join us.

Maybe coming here was a bad idea. Who really needs a fourth member anyway?

Still, I came up with a plan to help us work on dealing with being watched. I made a fake Minecraftian! I put together a few blocks of wood with a pumpkin on the top, carving a little face into it so it looked almost real.

"There," I said, as I placed the figure in front of us before we started our morning rehearsal. "That's our audience and it's going to be staring at us all the way through our rehearsal, so we're just going to have to deal with it."

Even though I knew that it was a fake Minecraftian, it was hard to keep my nerves under control as we sang in front of it. Those eyes, watching us all the time!

"I don't like this," said Phil after we'd finished our first song. "It creeps me out having someone watching us like that. I just want to go over to that statue and BAM!"

"That's exactly why we need to do this," I pointed out. "If you're feeling like this with just a statue watching, what's it going to be like with a proper audience? We need to get used to being watched before the show because once word gets out about how amazing we are, you just know that Minecraftians are going to want to come and watch. It's bad for business when you kill your audience."

"I suppose so," said Phil grudgingly.

"Come on, you two. Get into place." Zach hurried us along. "I want to get back on the road and find another Enderman to join our group. I hate being in the Overworld. The sooner we can go home and start building our theater, the better."

Phil and I took our positions next to Zach and started to hum the opening bars to *All the world belongs to Endermen. (No, really, it does.)*

I must admit that it was hard to keep focused with the statue watching. Everywhere we went, its eyes seemed to follow us. But we managed to get all the way through the number without making any serious mistakes and as we worked through our way through the show, the three of us gradually relaxed and almost forgot that we were being watched.

"That wasn't so bad, was it?" I smiled when we'd finished. "We'll be able to perform in front of a real audience in no time!"

Day 14

The forest gave way to swampland, disgusting boggy land filled with spooky noises and terrible smells, but there was still no sign of any Endermen. In fact, we didn't really come across anyone at all, not even some Minecraftians.

Maybe word was spreading that there were three Endermen making their way through the land and people were deliberately avoiding us. I could understand it, but it was most frustrating. If we could just find someone to give us directions, I know we could find the fourth member of our group in no time.

We carried our fake audience with us, slowing down our progress. Still, I'd spent so long working on Kevin, as Phil insisted on calling him, that it seemed a shame to leave him behind and it is really useful having him around to watch us rehearse. He seems to look at us disapprovingly when we get the dance moves wrong and I swear I heard him cheer when we finished our latest song *The Ender Dragon is the best dragon ever.* (A new song that Zach wrote especially for our debut show. He figured it couldn't hurt to dedicate a song to the Ender Dragon in the hope that he wouldn't set fire to us if he liked it.)

"Not bad, boys, but I think you could put a little more enthusiasm into your dancing."

The three of us looked at each other in surprise.

"Kevin? You can talk?" Phil crept forward to take a closer look as Zach and I shrugged at each other.

"Sheesh. I thought Enderman were supposed to be intelligent."

Phil jumped back as a witch stepped out from behind Kevin. He started to shake as she moved past him, but she waved him off. "Calm down, Enderboy. I'm not going to stare at you. I'm not really all that interested in watching Endermen roaming around. You've seen one of them walk, you've seen them all."

"But we weren't walking. We were dancing," I pointed out.

"So you'll want people to watch you perform then," she countered. "Not much good singing and dancing all by yourselves. You people." She cackled and shook her head.

"Yeah, well, we're working up to that," said Zach, folding his arms defiantly. "That's why we've got Kevin here."

The witch burst out laughing. "And now I've seen it all. Endermen singing to a stuffed pumpkin. I'd tell my friends, but no one would believe me."

The three of us blushed and moved about shiftily, not enjoying being laughed at.

"Anyway," she went on. "Aren't you a bit far from home? We don't usually get many Endermen around here."

My heart sank when I heard that. "That's annoying because that's exactly why we're here. We're looking for another Enderman to join our band."

"Why?" The witch scoffed. "Actually, don't answer that. I'm amazed that there are three of you daft enough to try and sing. Everyone knows that Endermen don't sing."

"Oh yeah? Let's show her! One, two, three, four!"

I started singing the introduction to my favorite song, *Who's that? It's an Enderman!* It had a really catchy riff and with Zach's vocals over Phil's beatboxing, you couldn't help but tap your feet to the beat.

I could see the witch's head start to nod, then her whole body sway from side to side before she started dancing, the music taking over so that she had to dance.

When the last notes faded away, she started applauding. "OK, you've convinced me. You boys have got talent! What's the name of your band? I want to tell all my friends that I saw you before you were famous."

We looked at each other. We hadn't actually chosen a name for ourselves yet.

"Er… The Enderman Four," I finally said.

"But there's only three of you," she pointed out.

"Not for long," I replied. "I just know that somewhere up here there's an Enderman waiting to join us. Maybe you could help us find them?"

"Not me!" The witch shook her head. "I like it here in my swamp. I'm not joining you on some hare-brained scheme."

"We could give you front row seats to our show," I pleaded.

"I'm not leaving the swamp. Minecraftians have a nasty habit of attacking witches when they see them, and I'm not in the mood for a fight." A thoughtful look came over her face. "However, there is a spell I could cast to help you find more Endermen. Would that be worth a front row seat?"

I grinned. "Definitely!"

Day 15

We spent the night camped outside the witch's hut. The sooner we're out of the swamp, the better. It really is disgusting here. My feet are really wet from wading through swamp water and I've got a headache from all the animal noises. There are creatures called pigs here, and they are stupidly noisy.

Oh for the order and calm of The End!

"Right, then. I'm going to cast this spell in exchange for front row tickets to your debut show, OK?" The witch came out of her hut carrying a cauldron and enchanted book.

"Yes, you can have one ticket for the show," I confirmed.

"One?" she screeched. "I want four!"

Zach shrugged. "Fine. Have four. Just make sure you warn all your friends not to stare at any Endermen who aren't on the stage. We can't be responsible if they start a fight."

"We're not stupid," the witch sneered. "Unlike some people I could mention."

Phil blushed. He was never going to live down the fact that he thought that Kevin was talking to him.

"All right. I need absolute silence for this spell to work. So no singing – you got that?"

She looked sharply at Zach, who stopped humming immediately.

The witch started throwing ingredients into her cauldron, muttering a spell.

Eye of spider, rabbit's foot,

Add some sugar and tree root,

Stir it round, one, two, three,

Show me where the Enders be!

There was a small explosion and a puff of purple smoke. She leaned forward, staring into the cauldron. The three of us craned our necks, trying to get a good look at the spell result.

"You need to go south," she said at last. "When you reach the extreme hills, go west and you should find an Enderman before too long. Of course, whether he'll want to join your little band of merry men is another matter completely and not something I can see for you. My spell is good, but it's not that good."

"It's good enough! Thank you! Thank you! Thank you!"

I could have hugged the witch, but she smelled of swamp water, so instead we all three shook her hands before setting off to the south, wanting to find our new band member as quickly as possible.

Day 16

"How long is it going to take us to get out of this blasted swamp?" whined Phil. "I'm tired of having wet feet all the time."

"Stop your complaining," snapped Zach, "and suck it up. We're Endermen! We can deal with anything."

"I still don't understand why we can't just teleport to where we want to go," grumbled Phil.

"We've been over this before," I sighed. "We can't teleport to somewhere we haven't been. We might end up in the middle of a hill or a lake and then we'll lose sight of each other, and who knows how long it will take for us to get back together again? I know this is a nuisance, but it's the only way. Besides, if we teleport, we might miss the Enderman we're looking for. We could jump straight over them, and then we'll waste even more time hunting around for them. Walking might take a long time, but in the long run, it's quicker."

"Shh!" Zach held up a hand for silence. "I'm sure I just heard something."

We all stopped walking and stood still as statues, not even daring to breathe.

A few moments later, Zach shook his head. "Whatever it is, it's gone."

"It's probably just an animal," Phil said.

"Maybe," Zach said, but I could tell that he wasn't convinced.

Now that he'd put the idea into my head, I couldn't shake the feeling that we were being watched. I could feel myself trembling with rage at the idea, but without knowing who was watching and where they were hiding, I couldn't go on the attack.

It was enough to make any Enderman nervous.

Day 17

"Somebody is definitely watching us," hissed Zach after we'd finished singing our first song of the morning. "I could see the bushes moving over there."

Phil started shaking, getting ready to fight. "Whoever he is, he's going to regret trying to take us on."

"Wait." I put out a hand to calm him down. "Let's not be too hasty. If Zach's right, this person has been following us for at least a couple of days, which means he's been watching us all this time and no harm has come to us. I say we wait a little bit longer before attacking, see what they want. If nothing else, this is good practice for when we have an audience. Poor old Kevin is looking a little worse for wear after all."

After a few days on the trail, Kevin's head was leaning to one side and he wasn't smelling too fresh. It was becoming harder to pretend that he was a real audience.

"All right," said Phil, making a visible effort to calm himself down. "I won't do anything to whoever is watching, but if we get ambushed in the middle of the night, don't say that I didn't warn you."

Day 18

"I don't like this one little bit," muttered Zach as we took our places for one of the dance numbers. "It's fine saying that we need to get used to an audience, but when we perform, they're going to be sitting right in front of us where we can see them. Having someone sneaking around in the bushes is a completely different matter. I don't care what you say, Eli. We need to find out who it is. For all we know, they could be trying to figure out our weak spots so they can attack."

"All right." I had to admit that I was also becoming disturbed by the idea that someone – maybe more than one person – was circling us without being seen. "You think our watcher is behind that bush over there?" I indicated with my eyes, trying not to give away the fact that we were talking about them.

Zach nodded.

"All right. Zach, you teleport behind them. Phil, you go over to that side and I'll walk straight at them, pretending that I'm just going for a little stroll. We'll have them surrounded. We'll ask them what they're doing and if we don't like the answer, we'll-"

"Obliterate them!" finished Zach, nodding in satisfaction.

"You're right, Eli! We did forget that... thing!" Phil said loudly so the person watching would hear. "I'll just go back and get it." He headed off down the path so he could go round to the side of the spy.

When he was gone, Zach called after him, "Wait a minute, Phil! I'll come with you!" He disappeared as he teleported off, supposedly to meet Phil, but really so that he could creep up behind the watcher, leaving me behind.

"I'm just going to go over here," I said, whistling a little to make myself look as innocent as possible.

I wandered over to the bush Zach had said was where the person was hiding.

"A-ha!" I jumped over the bush just as Zach appeared behind and pounced on our watcher, while Phil came round from the side.

"I looked all around," Phil said. "I couldn't see anyone else. I think this is the only one."

"Good. So who do we have here?"

Zach pulled the watcher to his feet and we all gasped at what we saw.

An Enderman!

Day 19

Robert is the strangest Enderman I've ever met. He's really short for a start, half the height of the three of us. There's something not quite right about the way he looks, and he doesn't talk like an Enderman either.

"So tell us again what you were doing in the bushes?" I asked him over breakfast.

"I've been following you for ages, ever since I first heard you sing," Robert explained. "But I was too shy to approach you and ask if I could join you. You're all so good, I didn't think you'd want a little runt like me in the band."

"Yes, you are really small for an Enderman," said Zach, giving Robert a shove to show how easily he could be pushed around.

"I'm not sure that we want someone in the group who's really shy," I told him. "After all, we've got a show to do in a few days. If you're too shy to come up and talk to us, how are you going to be able to get up on stage and sing in front of the Ender Dragon?"

"The Ender Dragon?" gasped Robert. "You're performing for the Ender Dragon?"

I nodded. "Yes. And you know what he's like if he doesn't like what you're doing. Are you really up for the challenge?"

"Are you kidding?" said Robert. "It's always been my dream to sing in front of the Ender Dragon! Could you imagine what it would be like, knowing that he enjoyed your music? It's the best thing that could happen. I'd be happy for the rest of my life if I just got the chance to stand in front of him and sing."

Zach pulled a face behind Robert's back. I could tell he didn't really believe what he was saying.

"All right," I said. "If you want a chance to sing for the Ender Dragon, then you're going to have to show us what you can do. Sing us your favorite song."

The three of us sat back as Robert took a nervous breath before starting, our hands hovering over our ears in case he turned out to be terrible.

When he'd finished singing, the three of us sat there in silence, unable to speak after what we'd just heard.

"You're perfect!" cried Zach at last, breaking the spell of silence as he jumped up to shake Robert's hand. "You're just what we need! You're in the band!"

"Hey! Shouldn't we talk about it first?" protested Phil.

"What's to talk about? He's amazing! Or are you seriously saying that you wouldn't have someone as good as Robert singing with us?"

Phil mumbled and grumbled, but it was obvious that he was just being silly.

There was no question about it. We'd found our fourth member!

"Well, it looks like the witch was wrong," I said. "We didn't even get as far as the Extreme Hills. I wonder why she didn't find Robert with her spell?"

"Pah!" spat Zach. "She was a witch. Everyone knows you can't trust witches."

"Does that mean that we don't have to give her front row seats?" asked Phil.

"What do you think?" sneered Zach.

Day 20

The jump back to The End was very odd. Usually, the more Endermen there are, the easier the journey, but this time, something seemed to be holding us back, as if one of us wasn't doing their job properly and it took a couple of attempts before we finally arrived at the point where we left.

"Phew! That was tough!" exclaimed Phil.

"Yeah. I hope we work together better than that for the show," said Zach. "There's not long now before opening night and we've still got a theater to build."

"I'm sure we can get some of the others to help us with the building," I said brightly. "We just need to figure out where we're going to put the stage."

"We've got a bigger problem than that," said Robert. "There's hardly any building resources here. I had no idea there was so little here."

"What do you mean?" Zach looked at him, a puzzled frown wrinkling his forehead. "This is what it's always been like here. It hasn't changed for over 400 years."

"Oh yeah." Robert laughed awkwardly. "It's just that I've been gone for so long, I'd forgotten, that's all. The island seemed bigger in my head."

"We're just going to have to teleport in extra blocks," said Phil. "As long as we keep the stage area small, it shouldn't be too much of a problem. Let's go through the show and mark out on the floor just how much space we need. Then we can start shipping in resources."

"Good idea."

As we started running through the show, Robert proved himself to be even better than he was in the audition. Although the songs were new to him, he picked things up really quickly and you could barely tell that he was new.

We were really lucky to have found him.

Day 21

Preparations for the show were really taking off. Zach had managed to persuade a few of the Endermen to help us build our stage. By persuade, I mean threaten to beat them up, but it meant that we had all the extra support we needed to get things done quickly.

We all agreed that we'd teleport up to Minecraftia, gather some wood and come back down again, adding it to the growing stage area before heading back up to get more. We were also putting together a basic frame so that we could have some curtains we could pull back when the show started, to bring in that dramatic effect.

"Come on, Robert," I said to our new member. "Let's teleport up and get some wood. It won't take long."

"Actually, I was thinking that I'd just stay here and build, if that's all right," Robert replied. "It's just that I've been away from home for so long that I'm really enjoying being here and I can't bear the thought of leaving again, even if it's just for a short while."

I smiled sympathetically. "I understand. All right then. You can start putting the stage together. You know how we want it, so I'll leave you in charge while I'm gone. Make sure that the other Endermen make a nice, flat stage. I don't want any nasty falls on the night."

"No problem," smiled Robert. "I'll make sure you get the best stage ever made!"

"There's something not quite right about that Enderman," muttered Zach, as I left Robert to his building.

"Who, Robert?" I looked back at where he was happily directing some Endermen to put their blocks down. "He's just spent a little bit too long in the Overworld, that's all. Give him a few days back home and you won't notice the difference between him and everyone else – apart from his amazing singing voice that is!"

"Maybe."

Zach continued to watch Robert suspiciously, and I had a horrible feeling that he wasn't going to leave Robert alone now that he'd decided he was a bit different.

Why wasn't it easy to put together the first Enderman band in history?

Day 22

The stage was almost complete and Robert had proven to be a big help. He seemed to have a knack for building, which was great since everyone else was absolutely useless. You'd tell them to put a block in a certain place and they'd throw it away or put things on top of each other instead of next to each other. Without Robert, it would have been a complete disaster.

Endermen don't usually create things, you see. We're very happy just wandering around The End, making sure that everything is safe and nobody bothers the Ender Dragon and anyway, there weren't many resources so it wasn't worth trying to build anything.

Robert was a natural builder. Under his directions, we didn't just have our flat stage with curtains. We had a dressing room and a special seat just for the Ender Dragon. It looked even better than I'd imagined.

I'd seen him disappear into the dressing room and I went to follow him, wanting to thank him for all his hard work, but when I opened the door, I couldn't believe what I saw.

"Robert! What? Who? I mean, what?"

The Robert I knew had disappeared, and in his place was a normal Minecraftian. He looked at me in shock and I could feel myself trembling at the thought that a lowly Minecraftian would dare to stare at me like that, especially after he'd fooled us all for so long.

He dropped his gaze, focusing on the floor. "I'm sorry, I'm sorry, I'm sorry," he whimpered, holding his hands up in surrender. "I didn't mean to lie to you."

Looking around to make sure that nobody else had seen Robert like this, I stepped into the room and shut the door behind me. "You've got five seconds to tell me what's going on before I attack," I said grimly. "Five, four..."

"Please don't hurt me!" he begged. "It's just that I heard you singing one morning. I'd never heard anything like it. When I saw that it was a group of Endermen, I couldn't believe it. Who knew that Endermen could sing? I desperately wanted to join your group, but I knew that if I asked you to let me in, you'd just fight me off. I couldn't bear to go away and never hear you sing again, so I came up with a plan to disguise myself as an Enderman. I figured that you wouldn't mind one of your own watching you, but I wasn't sure that my disguise was good enough to fool you, so I kept hiding while I watched you, studying how you moved and how you talked, so that it would be easier to pretend that I was one of you. When I heard you saying to the witch that you were looking for someone to join the band, I couldn't believe it. I love singing and it would be the biggest honor to sing with you, but if I wasn't sure if my disguise would fool you, how could I be sure that it would be good enough for the whole of The End? But then you found me and I didn't have any choice. I had to pretend I was an Enderman."

"And when were you going to tell me the truth?"

"After the show," came the reply. "I thought that if we did really well, then you'd forgive me for lying about who I am. And if we didn't…" He shrugged. "The Ender Dragon would make sure it wouldn't matter."

I thought for a moment, unsure of what to do. If the Endermen knew that there was a Minecraftian in our midst, he was in big trouble.

"Eli? Robert? Where are you?"

"Quick! Put your costume back on," I ordered. "Zach's coming and if he finds you like this, you really will be in danger."

Robert quickly threw his disguise on, just in time. Zach came into the dressing room. "There you are! I've been looking for you two all over the place. The stage is all finished and it's time to run through the show. Thanks to Robert, if we pull the curtains, nobody will be able to see what we're doing until opening night."

"We'll be right there," I replied. "I was just helping Robert learn some of the words."

"OK, well, I'm going to get Phil and then we need to get started. Every second counts, people!"

He disappeared off and I turned to face Robert.

"Your secret is safe with me," I said. "For the time being at least. But we're going to talk some more about this, OK?"

"Of course," nodded Robert, relieved.

Day 23

We rehearsed from the moment we woke up until it was time to go to bed, so I didn't get a chance to talk to Robert. So far, nobody else seems to know his secret, but now that I know that he's a Minecraftian, it's really obvious he's not an Enderman, and I've seen Zach watching him suspiciously.

I need to do something. If we lose Robert, it'll ruin everything. There isn't enough time to find a replacement and without the four of us, the show will be a flop.

Day 24

"Come with me." I grabbed Robert and dragged him into the dressing room, locking the door behind me. "I'm going to give you some lessons in being an Enderman. I've been watching you and if you keep on behaving the way you have been, someone is going to figure out the truth. Zach has already asked me if everything is all right and despite the way he looks, he's really not stupid. There's only so many times I can try and explain things by saying you spent too long in Minecraftia."

Robert turned pale. "Tell me what to do," he begged. "We've come too far now. I can't get caught."

"Right. Well the first problem is the way you walk. Enderman glide along smoothly like this." I showed him. "Your movements are too jerky. You need to slow things down."

Robert tried to walk like an Enderman.

"Better, better," I nodded. "But you're still not standing the way that Endermen do."

I spent the next hour coaching Robert on Enderman behavior and by the time we had to go back to rehearsals, he was a lot better.

"I guess that's the advantage of being a performer," I smiled. "You already know how to put on a show."

"You have no idea!" Robert grinned back.

Day 25

"Well, you know what they say," remarked Phil glumly. "A bad dress rehearsal means a good first night. That's got to be true, hasn't it?"

"This was a bad idea," said Zach angrily. "I don't know why I agreed to get involved with you losers. I should have known this was a stupid idea. Now I'm going to have the Ender Dragon mad at me. How could you have been so stupid, Eli? You know that we go to the left at the start of *Wiggle like an Enderman*!"

"Me?!" I exclaimed. "What about you? You wrote the songs and you STILL can't remember the words! At least I can say that I know all the songs backwards."

"Guys! Guys!" Robert stepped between me and Zach, seeing that we were about to start fighting. "It's pointless having a go at each other like this. We're never going to work like a team if all we do is fight. Anyway, it doesn't matter if we get it wrong. Nobody has seen the show before. How is the audience supposed to know that you should have gone left? Just smile and keep singing and nobody will know any different."

"I suppose," shrugged Zach. "Too late to do anything about it now anyway."

"Exactly," said Robert patiently. "So let's just go from the top and pretend that the last hour didn't happen. We can do this, guys! We're the Enderman Four, remember?"

"Yeah. About that," Zach drawled. "I think that's a stupid name. I think Zach and the Endermen has a much better ring to it. Don't you?"

"Zach and the Endermen?" I raised my eyebrows. "If it's going to be named after any of us, it should be me. I'm the one who put the band together, after all."

"Oh yeah? Well I write the songs. You wouldn't have any show if it wasn't for me."

Zach and I squared up to each other and Robert stepped between us once again.

"Guys, I've got it!"

We all turned round to look at Phil.

"We can be The Enders."

"The Enders." Zach said it slowly, rolling the words around his mouth as he thought about it. "I like it."

Robert and I nodded. "Me too," Robert said.

"So it's settled then," said Phil. "The Enders it is. Now can we get back to work and quit fighting?"

Day 26

Word had spread about our show, and all the Endermen who'd gone up to the Overworld were teleporting back, all desperate to see the show. Phil predicted that they'd only come back to watch us being eaten by the Ender Dragon, but there's no way that's going to happen.

All day, all you could hear was the little pop of teleporting Endermen as more and more arrived for the show. The theater was going to be packed!

"There he is! He'll tell you!"

I was just checking that the curtain was working when I heard the screech of the witch who'd cast the spell to find the other Endermen.

"Right. You. Tell this… person that my sisters and I have front row seats for your show. He's saying that we're not on his list, so we can't have our seats."

I looked over at Ted, the Enderman who'd been put in charge of making sure that everyone was sitting where they were supposed to do, leaving plenty of space for the Ender Dragon to have the best view. He had a plan of the theater and was marking down the names of everyone in the places allocated to them. "Sorry, Eli," he shrugged. "Zach told me that she can't have her seats. Something about a spell she did for you that went wrong?"

"My spell went wrong?" The witch's voice seemed to go up two octaves. "I'll have you know that my spells are never wrong!"

"Yes, well, Zach told me that you'd sent him off on some wild goose chase when the Enderman he needed was right there all along."

"That's a lie! There's no way that an Enderman was anywhere near the swamp!"

I gulped. This wasn't good. The witch was going to get Robert into serious trouble if I didn't shut her up.

"Look, this whole show was my idea in the first place," I said soothingly. "You were very kind to us in the swamp and no matter what Zach thinks happened, there's plenty of space for everyone. Give the witch and her sisters the seats on either side of the Ender Dragon."

"The Ender Dragon?" Now it was the witch's turn to gulp. "Now wait a minute. You didn't say anything about us having to sit with the Ender Dragon."

"I'm sorry, but those are the only front row seats left. If that's not fine with you, then I'm sure that Ted will find you somewhere else with a good view. We want you to be comfortable and happy after all."

"Yes, well, I think that somewhere else might be a good idea. Besides, I always hurt my neck if I sit too close to the stage," the witch sniffed. "You end up having to lean back to see everything. I think somewhere else would be the best idea."

"Great." I let Ted lead her away to find somewhere else for her to sit and couldn't keep back the sigh of relief that escaped me.

Now Zach wouldn't wonder why I'd insisted on letting the witch sit at the front, and she was happy with the seats she'd got. That was one crisis avoided. Now we just had to get through the show tomorrow and everything would be fine.

Day 27

"There are so many people!" squeaked Phil, looking through the curtains at the audience gathering on the other side. "I had no idea there were so many Endermen in the world! It looks like they've all come back to The End just to watch our show."

"Just as they should," nodded Zach. "It's going to be the best the world has ever seen. They're going to be talking about this night for centuries to come. Our names are going to go down in history, boys!"

"Are you ready?" Tom, the Enderman put in charge of the curtain called to us from the side of the stage. "The Ender Dragon has just arrived and you don't want to keep him waiting."

I peered out through the curtains and could see the Ender Dragon curling up in the space we'd left for him. We certainly didn't want him to wait. He had a tendency to start eating people when he got bored.

"Places, everyone!" I called. The four of us went to our spots, our backs to the audience. I nodded to Tom and he pulled the curtain open as the Endermen started cheering, just like in my dream.

"Doo be doo be doo!" Robert started singing the bassline to our opening number, *Endermen are people too,* and as the rest of us gradually joined in with him, we slowly spun round to face our audience.

The show had begun!

Everyone sat in stony silence as we moved about the stage, perfectly in time with each other. Clearly what people said was true – our dress rehearsal might have been a disaster, but the show was going well. This was the best we'd ever done and when the last few notes of *Endermen are people too* died away, the audience burst into loud applause, cheering, yelling, and stamping their feet on the ground. Even the Ender Dragon looked happy for once.

Robert and I grinned at each other, as we launched into our second song.

This was a fast song with complicated dance moves, but everything was going well until suddenly, Robert pulled out a sword he'd hidden in his costume. "Death to the Ender Dragon!" he yelled, as he launched himself into the audience.

For a moment, everyone froze, but as Robert's first hit landed squarely on the Ender Dragon's nose, chaos erupted. Screams split the air as Endermen scrambled to get to safety, knowing that the Ender Dragon wouldn't care who got hurt as he defended himself.

"I *told* you there was something strange about Robert!" cried Zach as he fled. "We should never have trusted him!"

Phil quickly followed and I stood in the middle of the stage, watching as my former bandmate tried his best to fight the biggest, meanest, nastiest creature in the whole of Minecraftia.

He was doing well, making the most of his surprise attack, but it was obvious that he was outclassed and it was only a matter of time before the Ender Dragon had him for breakfast.

I had no time to think about what I was doing. Instinct kicked in and I raced forward, grabbing hold of Robert and teleporting him away.

The screams faded into the distance and the world turned black.

Day 28

"What were you thinking?" I was so mad at Robert. I couldn't remember when I'd last been so angry. "Attacking the Ender Dragon? By yourself? Ruining the show? All that hard work for nothing! I thought we were friends."

"We *are* friends!" protested Robert. "But I couldn't tell you what I was planning. I didn't want to get you into trouble, and I didn't want you to try and stop me. But I thought you'd be on my side. You've always said how much you hated the Ender Dragon, so I thought you'd be happy that someone was going to get rid of him. All the Endermen would be free to do whatever they wanted. You could sing to your heart's content, transform The End into somewhere that all Minecraftians want to see for its amazing entertainment. You told me that Endermen are just misunderstood. This could have been the perfect opportunity to show the world how talented you guys really are."

I sighed and shook my head. "That may be true, but it doesn't matter now. You didn't kill the Ender Dragon. You should have known that it's impossible to do it by yourself.

Many Minecraftians have tried, but none of them have ever succeeded."

"I kind of hoped you guys would join in and help me." Robert had the decency to look embarrassed.

"Endermen don't fight the Ender Dragon. Ever. It doesn't matter what the circumstances," I said. "If you'd told me what you were planning, I could have told you that and saved you the trouble. As it is, now that I've saved you, I can't ever go back home. I'm stuck here in the Overworld."

"I'm really sorry, Eli. I didn't think."

"No. You didn't."

Day 29

"I have a plan!" announced Robert brightly.

"Not another one," I groaned. "Your last one went so well... not."

"Yes, but this one really is a good plan," he assured me. "After all that time working together practicing all those songs, it seems a shame to waste all that effort. We should go on a tour of Minecraftia, performing for everyone. It would be amazing! Nobody's ever seen an Enderman sing before. I know that everyone would want to see you. We could ask people to give us diamonds and emeralds if they liked our songs, and we could use the money to build a theater. Didn't you say that you wanted to have a theater named after you? This is your chance!"

I considered what he was saying. "It's not a bad idea," I said at last. "You're right. I did want a theater with my name on it. But do you really think that people will want to see an Enderman sing?"

Robert just looked at me. "Are you kidding?" he laughed. "I guarantee you that people will be lining up for miles! Everyone is so scared of Endermen that they'll love the chance to be able to look at one without being attacked, and that's before they hear how amazing your singing is. OK, so we're going to have to change some of the harmonies because there's only two of us, but I still reckon people will be amazed when they see you sing. So what do you say? Are we partners?"

He held out his hand for me to shake, a hopeful expression on his face.

At last, I reached out and took his hand. "Partners."

Day 30

"Right, so I've got a map of Minecraftia and I've started plotting out a route for our world tour." Robert spread the map out on the floor in front of me and I looked at it, amazed that there were so many interesting places to visit.

"These little dots are villages," he went on, "but they're often defended by iron golems and it might be a good idea to wait until we're well known before we try walking into a village. We don't want people to think that you're going in to attack them before you've had a chance to sing."

"No, we most definitely don't."

"So I think that what we need to do is set up on the road just outside the village so that anyone passing will be able to stop and watch. Then, once people see that we're musicians, we can try and move into town where we should be able to make more money."

As he continued to talk, I found it difficult to focus on what he was saying. Much as I liked the idea of singing my way around Minecraftia, after just one day away, I was missing my fellow Endermen. Much as Zach and Phil could be annoying at times, we'd been a team. A good team. Things weren't going to be the same without them.

"Oh and just one more thing." Robert grinned as he rolled up the map and tucked it into his backpack. "I've decided that this isn't going to work as a duo. We need a couple of other Endermen to sing with us."

I sighed. "That's where all the trouble started. Last time someone decided to bring some more Endermen into the group, it ended up with a certain person trying to kill the Ender Dragon."

"Well luckily for you, we don't have to go anywhere to find more Endermen. They've come to us."

"What do you mean?"

Robert moved aside as Zach and Phil stepped out from behind some trees.

"Zach! Phil! What are you guys doing here?"

"What – you thought we'd let you go off touring the world without us?" said Phil.

"Besides," Zach added. "Nobody would believe us when we said we didn't know what Robert's plans were. We didn't really have much of a choice. We had to get out of The End or be eaten by the Ender Dragon."

"Although I have to say that the look on the dragon's face when he realized that you'd taken Robert to the Overworld was hilarious!" giggled Phil.

"Let's see if we've still got it," said Zach. "One, two, one, two, three, four!"

As the four of us started singing, I couldn't have been happier. The Enders were back together again, and we were going to be the most famous Endermen Minecraftia had ever seen.

Printed in Poland
by Amazon Fulfillment
Poland Sp. z o.o., Wrocław

58863854R00047